PHANTOM OF THE OPERA

MEDLEY FOR VIOLIN

ARRANGED BY

Lindsey Stirling

T0066250

To access audio visit:
www.halleonard.com/mylibrary

7214-6874-4485-6960

Cover photo by Devin Graham

ISBN 978-1-4950-2131-2

Jon Vriesacker, violin

Audio Arrangements by Andrew Horowitz

Produced and Recorded by Jake Johnson at Paradyme Productions

HAL•LEONARD®
CORPORATION
7777 W. BLUEMOUND RD. P.O. BOX 13819 MILWAUKEE, WI 53213

Visit Hal Leonard Online at
www.halleonard.com

PHANTOM OF THE OPERA MEDLEY

Violin

Music by ANDREW LLOYD WEBBER
Lyrics by CHARLES HART
Additional Lyrics by RICHARD STILGOE and MIKE BATT
Violin arranged by Lindsey Stirling

THE PHANTOM OF THE OPERA

Somberly (♩ = 90)

Gently, sustained, as if in the distance

Quicker, with intensity (♩ = 158)

ANGEL OF MUSIC
Music by ANDREW LLOYD WEBBER
Lyrics by CHARLES HART
Additional Lyrics by RICHARD STILGOE

THINK OF ME
Music by ANDREW LLOYD WEBBER
Lyrics by CHARLES HART
Additional Lyrics by RICHARD STILGOE

116   **Gently and sustained (♩ = 102)**

THE MUSIC OF THE NIGHT
Music by ANDREW LLOYD WEBBER
Lyrics by CHARLES HART
Additional Lyrics by RICHARD STILGOE

132   **Driving forward, with intensity (♩ = 133)**

THE PHANTOM OF THE OPERA

Quicker, with intensity (♩ = 158)

HAL•LEONARD® VIOLIN PLAY-ALONG

AUDIO ACCESS INCLUDED

The Violin Play-Along Series

Play your favorite songs quickly and easily!

Just follow the music, listen to the CD or online audio to hear how the violin should sound, and then play along using the separate backing tracks. The audio files are enhanced so you can adjust the recordings to any tempo without changing pitch!

1. Bluegrass
00842152 ....$14.99

2. Popular Songs
00842153 ....$14.99

3. Classical
00842154 ....$14.99

4. Celtic
00842155 ....$14.99

5. Christmas Carols
00842156 ....$14.99

7. Jazz
00842196 ....$14.99

8. Country Classics
00842230 ....$14.99

9. Country Hits
00842231 ....$14.99

10. Bluegrass Favorites
00842232 ....$14.99

11. Bluegrass Classics
00842233 ....$14.99

12. Wedding Classics
00842324 ....$14.99

13. Wedding Favorites
00842325 ....$14.99

14. Blues Classics
00842427 ....$14.99

15. Stephane Grappelli
00842428 ....$14.99

16. Folk Songs
00842429 ....$14.99

17. Christmas Favorites
00842478 ....$14.99

18. Fiddle Hymns
00842499 ....$14.99

19. Lennon & McCartney
00842564 ....$14.99

20. Irish Tunes
00842565 ....$14.99

21. Andrew Lloyd Webber
00842566 ....$14.99

22. Broadway Hits
00842567 ....$14.99

23. Pirates of the Caribbean
00842625 ....$14.99

24. Rock Classics
00842640 ....$14.99

25. Classical Masterpieces
00842642 ....$14.99

26. Elementary Classics
00842643 ....$14.99

27. Classical Favorites
00842646 ....$14.99

28. Classical Treasures
00842647 ....$14.99

29. Disney Favorites
00842648 ....$14.99

30. Disney Hits
00842649 ....$14.99

31. Movie Themes
00842706 ....$14.99

32. Favorite Christmas Songs
00102110 ....$14.99

33. Hoedown
00102161 ....$14.99

34. Barn Dance
00102568 ....$14.99

35. Lindsey Stirling
00109715 ....$19.99

36. Hot Jazz
00110373 ....$14.99

37. Taylor Swift
00116361 ....$14.99

38. John Williams
00116367 ....$14.99

39. Italian Songs
00116368 ....$14.99

40. Trans-Siberian Orchestra
00119909 ....$19.99

41. Johann Strauss
00121041 ....$14.99

42. Light Classics
00121935 ....$14.99

43. Light Orchestra Pop
00122126 ....$14.99

44. French Songs
00122123 ....$14.99

45. Lindsey Stirling Hits
00123128 ....$19.99

46. Piazzolla Tangos
48022997 ....$16.99

47. Light Masterworks
00124149 ....$14.99

48. Frozen
00126478 ....$14.99

49. Pop/Rock
00130216 ....$14.99

50. Songs for Beginners
00131417 ....$14.99

51. Chart Hits for Beginners – 2nd Ed.
00293887 ....$14.99

52. Celtic Rock
00148756 ....$14.99

53. Rockin' Classics
00148768 ....$14.99

54. Scottish Folksongs
00148779 ....$14.99

55. Wicked
00148780 ....$14.99

56. The Sound of Music
00148782 ....$14.99

57. Movie Music
00150962 ....$14.99

58. The Piano Guys – Wonders
00151837 ....$19.99

59. Worship Favorites
00152534 ....$14.99

60. The Beatles
00155293 ....$14.99

61. Star Wars: The Force Awakens
00157648 ....$14.99

62. Star Wars
00157650 ....$14.99

63. George Gershwin
00159612 ....$14.99

64. Lindsey Stirling Favorites
00159634..................$19.99

65. Taylor Davis
00190208..................$19.99

66. Pop Covers
00194642..................$14.99

67. Love Songs
00211896..................$14.99

68. Queen
00221964..................$14.99

69. La La Land
00232247..................$17.99

70. Metallica
00242929..................$14.99

71. Andrew Lloyd Webber Hits
00244688..................$14.99

72. Lindsey Stirling – Selections from Warmer in the Winter
00254923..................$19.99

73. Taylor Davis Favorites
00256297..................$19.99

74. The Piano Guys – Christmas Together
00262873..................$19.99

75. Ed Sheeran
00274194..................$16.99

77. Favorite Christmas Hymns
00278017..................$14.99

78. Hillsong Worship Hits
00279512..................$14.99

79. Lindsey Stirling – Top Songs
00284305..................$19.99

80. Gypsy Jazz
00293922..................$14.99

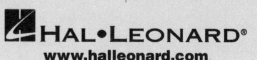

HAL•LEONARD®

www.halleonard.com